# An Invitation
# to Dance

# *An Invitation to Dance*

*T*he world of classical dance music is as varied as it is compelling. Ancient cultures, popular folk stories, stately occasions, romantic meetings, and social gatherings are all sources of inspiration for the great composers, and every mood is captured on this vibrant yet reflective volume. From the sultry seductiveness of Grieg's "Anitra's Dance" to Weber's formal *Invitation to the Dance*, or Borodin's exotic "Polovtsian Dances" to the delightful Minuet and Trio from Schubert's Fifth Symphony, you are invited to dance to your favorite tunes.

---

## THE LISTENER'S GUIDE – WHAT THE SYMBOLS MEAN

| THE COMPOSERS | THE MUSIC | THE INSPIRATION | THE BACKGROUND |
|---|---|---|---|
| Their lives... their loves.. their legacies... | Explanation... analysis... interpretation... | How works of genius came to be written | People, places, and events linked to the music |

# Contents

– 2 –
*The Bartered Bride: Act 3 (Dance of the Comedians)*
BEDŘICH SMETANA

– 4 –
*Peer Gynt, Suite No.1, Opus 46: Anitra's Dance*
EDVARD GRIEG

– 5 –
*Slavonic Dance No.8, Opus 46*
ANTONIN DVOŘÁK

– 6 –
*Mazurka in B-flat Major No.1, Opus 7*
FRÉDÉRIC CHOPIN

– 8 –
*Symphonie Fantastique: Second Movement (Un Bal)*
HECTOR BERLIOZ

– 10 –
*Tritsch Tratsch Polka*
JOHANN STRAUSS II

– 11 –
*España, Opus 165*
ISAAC ALBÉNIZ

– 14 –
*Invitation to the Dance*
CARL MARIA VON WEBER

– 15 –
*Symphony No.5 in B-flat Major: Third Movement*
FRANZ SCHUBERT

– 16 –
*Ancient Airs and Dances: Suite No.2 (Bergamasca)*
OTTORINO RESPIGHI

– 18 –
*Eugene Onegin: Act 3, Scene 1*
PYOTR TCHAIKOVSKY

– 20 –
*Wilson's Wilde/Mistress Winter's Jump*
MICHAEL PRAETORIUS

– 22 –
*La Gioconda: Act 3 (Dance of the Hours)*
AMILCARE PONCHIELLI

– 24 –
*Prince Igor: Act 2 (Polovtsian Dances)*
ALEXANDER BORODIN

BEDŘICH SMETANA *1824–1884*

# The Bartered Bride

## ACT 3
## (DANCE OF THE COMEDIANS)

This lively and acrobatic dance from the third act of Smetana's opera depicts the tumblers and jugglers of a traveling circus troupe. It is full of bold contrasts of mood, as heard in the strident orchestral outbursts, the racing violins, the playful woodwind, and the bold trumpet line with snare drum accompaniment. The dance is a blaze of swirling color and movement, expressing exuberance and festive spirit. Notice how, toward the end of the dance, the music pauses briefly to denote a moment of suspense in the acrobatic entertainment before proceeding to its dramatic final conclusion.

## IN A LIGHTER VEIN

 Before Smetana wrote *The Bartered Bride (below)*, many critics had labeled him a "Wagnerian," implying that he was incapable of writing anything light. The high spirits of this opera proved them wrong. The Czech composer aimed to give it a national character and based his story on Bohemian villagers and their simple, rustic existence. The opera received accolades from audiences, but the critics were

still unforgiving, with one Russian condemning it as "just about worthy of a gifted fourteen year old." In spite of this, a brilliant production in Vienna in 1892, followed by great performances in Chicago, London, and New York, secured its success.

## UNEASY COURTSHIP

 Smetana's courtship with his friend Katerina Kolárová was very different from the greedy ones he wrote about in this opera. Smetana *(right)* fell for Katerina as a teenager, but his

strong affections frightened her away, and he was not able to persuade her to marry him until he was twenty-five. Tragically, she died only nine years later of tuberculosis.

## TRAVELING CIRCUS

 *The Bartered Bride* centers on the arranged marriage of Marenka. Through a broker, her parents have arranged a match with Vasek, a simpleton. However, Marenka is in love with Jeník and Vasek falls for Esmerelda, a circus dancer. What follows is a merry tale of bribery, intrigue, and double-bluffs.

### KEY NOTES
The Bartered Bride is Smetana's most popular opera, even though it was not his personal favorite. After its 1892 Vienna production, it became Smetana's only opera to achieve success outside his native Bohemia.

## EDVARD GRIEG *1843–1907*

# *Peer Gynt*

### SUITE NO.1, OPUS 46:
### ANITRA'S DANCE

The seductive Oriental charm of "Anitra's Dance" is conveyed by the unusual combination of stringed instruments and a triangle. The graceful violin melody is set against a light pizzicato accompaniment in triple time. Sensuous chords give the dance a more sinister atmosphere, and we can sense Peer yielding to Anitra's charms. The dance ends as it began—with quiet violins as Anitra skips away, inviting Peer to follow.

## ANITRA'S CHARMS

At this point in Heinrik Ibsen's play—for which Grieg wrote the incidental music—the hero, Peer Gynt, has just encountered a group of Arabian girls at an oasis who hail him as a prophet. One of them, Anitra, the daughter of an Arabian chieftain, entertains Peer with this alluring dance, and they soon become lovers. But Peer comes to regret his encounter when the beguiling Anitra makes off with all his belongings.

### KEY NOTES

Peer Gynt *was first performed in 1876 in Christiana (now Oslo), Norway. Neither Ibsen nor Grieg was present but it was a big success— its opening run was only halted when a fire destroyed the scenery.*

## ANTONIN DVOŘÁK
*1841–1904*

# Slavonic Dance

### NO.8, OPUS 46

This is one of the best known of Dvořák's *Slavonic Dances*. The dramatic, forceful rhythm of this folk dance, with its emphasis placed firmly on the first and third beats of the bar, inspires the exciting gypsy atmosphere. A skipping passage introduces a contrasting second theme on the woodwind before the opening theme returns. This is followed by a broader melody on the strings and woodwind, which irresistibly captures the mood of the peasant dances of central Europe.

## THE NATIONALIST CAUSE

The Opus 46 set of *Slavonic Dances* (the first of two sets) was written and published in 1878, a year of intense nationalist fervor throughout southern and central Europe. Together with Smetana, Dvořák brought the folk music of his native Bohemia into the limelight, establishing it as a unique musical genre of the 19th century.

### KEY NOTES

The Slavonic Dances *were originally written as piano duets. It was only later that Dvořák made orchestral arrangements from them— the form in which they are best known.*

FRÉDÉRIC CHOPIN *1810–1849*

# *Mazurka in B-flat Major*

## NO.1, OPUS 7

The mood of the *Mazurka in B-flat Major* is one of great joy, which Frédéric Chopin conveys in a characteristically light and effortless fashion. The music skips gracefully from one phrase to the next, with a series of subtle inflections and delicate pauses in the rhythm. A slightly questioning passage returns twice to provide a short-lived contrast to the uplifting mood of the rest of the piece.

## NATIONAL ORIGINS

Frédéric Chopin's fifty-two mazurkas written for solo piano are probably the most famous versions of this traditional Polish dance. For Chopin, the national origins of the mazurka gave this dance particular personal significance, so he was able to bring remarkable levels of expression to his versions.

## THE MAZURKA

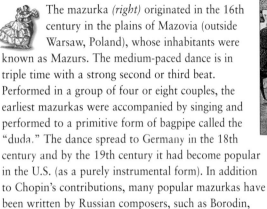

The mazurka *(right)* originated in the 16th century in the plains of Mazovia (outside Warsaw, Poland), whose inhabitants were known as Mazurs. The medium-paced dance is in triple time with a strong second or third beat. Performed in a group of four or eight couples, the earliest mazurkas were accompanied by singing and performed to a primitive form of bagpipe called the "duda." The dance spread to Germany in the 18th century and by the 19th century it had become popular in the U.S. (as a purely instrumental form). In addition to Chopin's contributions, many popular mazurkas have been written by Russian composers, such as Borodin, Glinka, and Tchaikovsky.

## A TRAGEDY FOR POLAND

During the time Chopin was writing this mazurka, in 1831, he received news that Warsaw had fallen to the Russians *(below)* after a year-long struggle. He was greatly saddened by the continuing troubles of his country and his nationalist feelings can be felt in his work.

### KEY NOTES

*The emphasis on the off-beat distinguishes the mazurka from the waltz. However, Chopin's mazurkas did not always stick to the traditional medium-paced form and were often much faster.*

### HECTOR BERLIOZ *1803–1869*

## *Symphonie Fantastique*

### SECOND MOVEMENT (UN BAL)

In this movement from Hector Berlioz's "Fantastic Symphony," the hero seeks to escape the torment of unrequited love by losing himself in the fun and excitement of the dance. The dazzling atmosphere of a ballroom is magnificently conveyed from the onset, while a dramatic build-up introduces the dance—a charming and carefree waltz. The pace quickens as the graceful string melody is enhanced by a harp. During the festivities, however, the central character is drawn back to the image of his beloved, as the waltz melody is combined with a musical *idée fixe*—a recurring short theme representing the hero's beloved.

## PLUNGED INTO A NIGHTMARE WORLD

Composed in 1830, the *Symphonie Fantastique*, subtitled "Episodes in the Life of an Artist," was the first great piece of French Romantic music. In his memoirs, Berlioz writes that the subject of this semi-autobiographical musical drama was his love for the Irish actress Harriet Smithson *(left)*, who was playing Ophelia in *Hamlet* in Paris at the time. The symphony's five-movement programme tells of a young musician who falls in love with the woman of his dreams. Driven to despair because she does not love him in return, the artist takes opium, which plunges him into a succession of dreams and nightmares. In one of the dreams he is marched to the guillotine, while in another he finds himself in a world inhabited by sorcerers and ghosts, as well as by his beloved in the form of a witch.

Above: *The ballroom scene from* Symphonie Fantastique *by the French artist Henri Fantin-Latour.*

## BERLIOZ THE ORCHESTRATOR

Berlioz *(left)* was highly aware of each instrument's unique ability to create a particular mood. In his writings on instrumentation, he explains how certain blends of instruments can create memorable moments. His own music is rich in color and texture through his skillful and imaginative orchestration. Berlioz was also a masterful orchestrator of other composers' works, including Weber's piano piece *Invitation to the Dance*—which is also included in this collection.

### KEY NOTES

Idée fixe ("fixed idea") was a medical term for a delusion resulting in abnormal actions. Berlioz, a former medical student, used it as a musical term, to describe the device of a recurring theme.

**JOHANN STRAUSS II** *1825–1899*

# *Tritsch Tratsch Polka*

T he *Tritsch Tratsch Polka* has always been one of Johann Strauss's most popular works. Strauss once stated that at one concert the audience demanded to hear it played an amazing thirty-eight times! The polka is a light and high-spirited dance in which the orchestra indulges in decorative runs, trills, and humorous flourishes. The brass and percussion are used to excellent effect, although the furious pace of the dance makes it very demanding on the players.

## CHITCHAT

The title for this polka comes from the German word *tratsch*, meaning gossip. *Tritsch* was added later simply to make the title resemble the English phrase "chitchat." Polkas made up an important part of the classical Viennese dance repertoire; many took their titles from girls' names—such as *Elise* and *Pepita*—though Strauss gave his rather more exciting titles, including the *Elektro-magnetische Polka* and the *Explosions Polka*.

### KEY NOTES

The Tritsch Tratsch Polka *became a big hit for the famous folk performer Moser, who used to tour the Viennese cafés performing with a popular Schrammel quartet, which consisted of two violins, a guitar, and an accordion.*

**ISAAC ALBÉNIZ** *1860–1909*

## *España*

### OPUS 165

Written for solo piano, this tango shows Isaac Albéniz's interest in Impressionist music—particularly that of Claude Debussy, who was perhaps his greatest single influence. It is more of a tango for the mind than for the dance floor: the lower instruments tentatively keep the music moving, while the questioning rhythm and delicate pauses lead us far from the drive and earthiness of the traditional dance band tango. But the feel and rhythm of the music is unmistakably Latin and typical of Albéniz's feeling for his cultural roots.

## THE RUNAWAY

Isaac Albéniz *(below)* was one of Spain's greatest musical figures. As a child, he showed enormous talent as a pianist, making his debut in Barcelona at the age of four. Soon he began running away from home to give concert tours. Once, after being placed on a train home by a friendly mayor, he switched trains and set off to tour the cities of Castile. On another occasion he ran away to tour Andalucia before heading off for South America as a stowaway. Restless and hardworking by nature, Albéniz never stayed in one city for long. Even in his final years, afflicted with kidney disease, he kept up his travels. He died at forty-nine and was posthumously awarded the Grand Cross of the *Légion d'honneur* by the French government.

## BEST WORK

Although Albéniz's *España* is justly famous, his *Iberia* suite is regarded as his crowning glory. The twelve pieces, recalling different regions of Spain, are distinguished by a complex technique in which the piano imitates the guitar or castanets.

## THE HABAÑERA

The tango is very similar to the habañera, a slow dance in two-four time with a characteristic syncopated rhythm, which was invented in the Cuban capital of Havana. Probably the most famous habañera is sung by Carmen *(left)* in Georges Bizet's opera of that name, which he adapted from a song by another Spanish composer, Sebastián Yradier. Debussy also wrote two habañeras, while Maurice Ravel uses one as the third movement of his orchestral work *Rapsodie Espagnole* ("Spanish Rhapsody").

## THE ORIGINS OF THE TANGO

The tango first became popular around the turn of the 20th century in the cities of Argentina, particularly in the poor areas of Buenos Aires. The dance's rise to international prominence was due largely to dance idol Carlos Gardel (1887–1935) who performed the tango throughout Europe during the 1920s. The exact origins of the tango, however, are unknown. One theory suggests that it was imported into America by African slaves who gave the name to their drums. The word then

became associated with the dance. Originally the tango was full of informal movements and tight embraces. But as it became more popular—in fashionable Parisian society, at the English theater, and in American restaurants, parties, and "tango teas"—it became increasingly formal. After 1907 it reached the highly stylized form favored by today's ballroom dancers.

## THE LATIN CRAZE

The 1930s brought a new interest in Latin American dancing. The rumba from Cuba was the first to reach New York, in 1931, followed by the Brazilian samba. Spurred on by Hollywood musicals, numerous Latin American dance forms began to gain popularity, including the bolero, cha cha (above), conga, and mambo.

"Cha-Cha-Cha BOOM!"
A CLOVER PRODUCTION · A COLUMBIA PICTURE

### KEY NOTES

The tango has been a source of inspiration for many 20th-century works, notably Stravinsky's Soldier's Tale and Walton's Façade.

OTTORINO RESPIGHI *1879–1936*

# Ancient Airs and Dances

## SUITE NO.2 (BERGAMASCA)

*A*ncient Airs and Dances comprises three suites. It consists of arrangements of pieces by earlier Italian composers and is an excellent example of Respighi's ingenuity in the handling of orchestration. The opening of "Bergamasca" immediately transports us into the Italian countryside where the folk are joyously dancing and singing. Respighi's colorful and highly imaginative use of instrumental sounds, such as the pizzicato strings, harp, and brass, greatly enhances the dance's uniquely fresh appeal.

### A PEASANT DANCE

*Bergamasca* is derived from a peasant dance from Bergamo in northern Italy. This particular one was originally written in 1650 by Italian composer Bernardo Gianoncelli.

## THE ETERNAL CHILD

Ottorino Respighi *(below)* was at his best when evoking idyllic or picturesque scenes in his orchestral music, as in his much-loved *Fontane di Roma* ("Fountains of Rome"). In later years, he returned to his first love—opera—but according to critics, his skill in handling dramatic or passionate themes rarely matched his talent for applying descriptive color, freshness, and lightness to his works. Perhaps this was because he always remained a child at heart. One of his greatest achievements was the opera *La bella addormentata nel bosco* ("The Sleeping Beauty in the Forest"), which was written for puppets and later adapted for child mimes with offstage voices.

## FASCIST ITALY

Italy's fascist regime under Mussolini *(right)* had a powerful influence on the arts. Although Respighi was a member of the new Italian Society of Modern Music set up by Italian composer Alfred Casella in 1917, he was opposed to futuristic styles of music, preferring to breathe new life into traditional forms rather than create new ones. He even signed a notorious manifesto attacking the progressive musical trends of the time.

Respighi has been accused of fascist tendencies in his own music, in particular his *Feste romane* ("Roman festivals"), but such uninhibited self-indulgence was probably more an expression of his exuberant naiveté than as a conscious political statement.

### KEY NOTES

*Apparently Respighi played* Ancient Airs and Dances *to his composition class, explaining that it was based on old lute pieces. According to his wife Elsa, this was the only time he referred to any of his own works in the classroom.*

PYOTR TCHAIKOVSKY
*1840–1893*

# Eugene Onegin

## ACT 3, SCENE I

An initial trumpet fanfare and a flourish on the strings opens this polonaise, which introduces us to formal St. Petersburg society. After the opening sequence, a much lighter middle section on the woodwind leads into a broad and more reflective passage on the cellos before the main polonaise returns. The piece ends with a treatment that is typical of the composer—a powerful, dramatic buildup leading to a rousing finish.

## FROM PEASANTS TO NOBILITY

The polonaise is a traditional Polish dance in triple time. Similar to the mazurka, it is characterized by a strong off-beat rhythm, often with the emphasis on the second beat. From its folk roots, where it was originally sung as well as danced, it became popular with the aristocracy in the 16th century and acquired a strong ceremonial feel. Chopin's thirteen piano polonaises are outstanding examples of this dance form.

## PUSHKIN'S INFLUENCE

 *Eugene Onegin* is based on a work by Russian poet Alexander Pushkin (1799–1837), which he modeled on Lord Byron's poem *Don Juan*. Pushkin's influence on Russian music was widespread. His poetry had a huge appeal, not only because of its extraordinary breadth and variety of characters, but also because of the musical appeal of its language. Among the more famous works directly inspired by Pushkin *(right)* are Glinka's *Ruslan and Lyudmila*, Mussorgsky's *Boris Godunov*, Rimsky-Korsakov's *The Golden Cockerel*, and two others by Tchaikovsky—*Mazeppa* and *The Queen of Spades*. Rachmaninov and Stravinsky also used Pushkin's verse as a source of inspiration.

## TATYANA'S HOLD

 Tchaikovsky's short-lived marriage closely mirrors the story of this opera. In 1877 he received a series of desperate love letters from an Antonina Milyukova, who claimed she knew him;

eventually he visited her to formally reject her advances. However, just before their meeting he had started work on *Eugene Onegin* and had fallen in love with the character of Tatyana *(left)*. He was deeply disturbed by Onegin's spurning of Tatyana after receiving a letter from her. As a result, a week after meeting her, he proposed marriage—an action he quickly came to regret.

### KEY NOTES

Tchaikovsky wrote ten operas, though he later destroyed two of them. Eugene Onegin, completed in 1878, is possibly the most successful of all his operatic works. It remains to this day his most-performed opera throughout the world.

**MICHAEL PRAETORIUS** *c.1571–1621*

# *Wilson's Wilde/Mistress Winter's Jump*

Although the German composer and arranger Michael Praetorius claimed that these tunes were "Französische Tänze" (French dances), their origins appear to date back to 16th-century England. Praetorius's charming arrangement utilizes many of the instruments that would have been used during this period, creating a truly authentic 16th-century sound. For instance, this piece features English and Flemish forms of the bagpipe (one of the oldest-known instruments still being played today).

## HIS LAST NAME

The name Praetorius is actually the Latinized form of Schultz that was adopted by many German composers of the 16th and 17th centuries.

## A VAST OUTPUT

Michael Praetorius *(below)* was born into a family of strict Lutherans. For most of his life he worked as a church organist in and around Frankfurt, composing and publishing church music. His

output was enormous and showed astounding creativity; it included a nine-volume collection, *Musae Sioniae*, containing over 1,200 pieces. Praetorius was largely self-taught and, although he dedicated his

life's work to sacred music, he produced many other forms of music, including arrangements of folk dances. In addition, he was an accomplished theorist. On his death, he left a sizable fortune, most of which was used to establish a foundation for the poor.

## MUSIC HISTORIAN

Praetorius was a thorough music historian, and his three-volume history of music, the *Syntagma musicum* ("Musical Collection"), is a comprehensive account of music theory. The first volume is on religious music. The second volume, regarded as the most important, is *De organographia* ("Writing for the Organ"). It gives a detailed account of the instruments of his day with forty-two illustrations *(right)*. The third volume concerns musical techniques.

### KEY NOTES

*While the French origin of Wilson's Wilde/Mistress Winter's Jump is doubtful, Praetorius's Suite de Voltes is an excellent example of early French folk dance.*

AMILCARE PONCHIELLI 1834–1886

# La Gioconda

## ACT 3 (DANCE OF THE HOURS)

"Dance of the Hours" is a ballet sequence taken from Amilcare Ponchielli's most popular opera. The music, which moves through a number of moods, symbolizes the eternal conflict between light and darkness. The opening theme represents dawn and is introduced by strings and harp, followed by birdlike flutters on the woodwind. A violin melody and woodwind responses with pizzicato accompaniment then establish a sprightly mood. A chime marks the change to darkness as the cellos take the lead. Sweeping strings and brass follow, ushering in a fast-paced dance as a finale to the piece.

### A SOLE REMINDER

From Ponchielli's numerous operas, only *La Gioconda* ("The Joyful Girl") is still in the modern repertoire. Even during his lifetime, his other works failed to gain a wide acclaim. His lack of recognition is due more to his passive personality rather than his talent.

## MUSICAL TALENTS

Amilcare Ponchielli *(right)* was born near Cremona, Italy. His musical talents were evident from an early age and he entered the Milan Conservatory at the age of nine, composing his first symphony a year later. After graduating with a diploma, he moved to Cremona itself, where he took up conducting and composing operas. Ponchielli struggled to achieve success at anything other than a local level. His meek disposition prevented him from moving out of the provinces to further his career—he was highly praised during his time at the Milan Conservatory, but it still took eighteen years for his work to be heard at a Milan theater. In May 1880, Ponchielli at last achieved fame when he was awarded the chair of composition at the Milan Conservatory. Among his most celebrated pupils were Puccini, whom he persuaded to write his first opera, and, for a short while, Mascagni. He died in Milan at age fifty-one and was mourned throughout Italy.

## LA GIOCONDA

Ponchielli *(left)* wrote *La Gioconda* as a four-act opera, based on Victor Hugo's play *Angelo, Tyran de Padoue* ("Angelo, the Tyrant of Padua"). First performed in Milan in 1876, the opera is set in 17th-century Venice and revolves around a street singer named Gioconda. "Dance of the Hours" is the entertainment put on by one of the characters, Alvise Badoero, for his guests.

### KEY NOTES

The most famous part of this piece was made into a popular song by the witty American performer Allan Sherman in 1963. Entitled Hello Muddah, Hello Faddah, the million-selling record humorously related a letter written by a young boy to his parents from summer camp.

## ALEXANDER BORODIN *1833–1887*

# Prince Igor

### ACT 2 (POLOVTSIAN DANCES)

The first of these Polovtsian Dances starts with a fast, spiralling of notes on the woodwind, accompanied by a broad string melody, while the horns and percussion add excitement. The dance that follows is introduced by the percussion and, by contrast, is much slower. Its strong, heavy rhythm wonderfully depicts the barbarous characters who capture Igor in this opera. This is followed by a quicker, bouncier dance. Four descending notes on strings provide an atmosphere of intrigue, which dissolves into the gentle and lyrical "Maidens' Dance." Finally, brief echoes from preceding sections bring the set to a momentous climax.

### ROYAL ENTERTAINMENT

The "Polovtsian Dances" form the ballet scene in Act 2 of *Prince Igor* at the point when the Polovtsian leader Khan Konchak entertains his prisoner Prince Igor with a series of Oriental dances.

## TWO STRINGS TO HIS BOW

Alexander Borodin *(right)* was the illegitimate son of the elderly Russian Prince Gedianov and his twenty-four-year-old mistress Madame Antonova. By the age of nine, he had learned to play the piano and flute and had already composed his first polka. But throughout his life, his interest in chemistry equalled that of music, and today he is remembered for his contributions to both professions. After graduating as a doctor of medicine in 1858, Borodin moved to Heidelberg, where he met his future wife Ekaterina Protopopova, a pianist who had considerable musical influence on him. In later years, Borodin suffered from declining health. He survived cholera at the age of fifty-two, but died suddenly of heart failure at a ball two years later, never completing *Prince Igor*. The masterpiece was finished by Glazunov and Rimsky-Korsakov.

## BACKGROUND RESEARCH

The story of Borodin's opera *Prince Igor* is set in the 12th century when nomadic people known as the Polovtsians *(left)* invaded southern Russia. The story, which concerns the capture of Prince Igor of Russia by the Polovtsians, was researched by the composer with his customary scientific thoroughness for authenticity.

### KEY NOTES

On returning to St. Petersburg in 1862, Borodin met Balakirev and became the fifth member of the nationalist group of composers known as "The Five," along with Cui, Mussorgsky, and Rimsky-Korsakov, who greatly encouraged Borodin in his music.

# *Credits &*
# *Acknowledgments*

## PICTURE CREDITS

Cover/Title and Contents Pages/IBC: Photonica/Paul VozdicAKG London: 7(tr), 10, 12(t), 16, 17(l & r), 19(r), 21(l); Bridgeman Art Library, London/Magyar Newzeti Galeria, Budapest (Karoly Lotz: A Village Wedding Feast): 5; Gavin Graham Gallery, London (A. Baumgartner-Stoiloff: Cossacks in a Winter Landscape): 7(bl); Royal Asiatic Society, London: 24; Corbis/Everett: 13(b); Mary Evans Picture Library: 11, 13(t), 25(tl); Steve Rumne:y 6; Fine Art Photographic Library (E & G. Klimt:A Theatrical Buffoon): 2; (Giacomo Mantegazza: A Harem Scene): 4; (Lucien Frank: Le Bal en Eté): 8; (George Goodwin Kilburne: Introduction at the Ball): 14; John Mitchell & Son, London (Pieter Breughel the Younger: The Wedding Dance): 20; Lebrecht Collection: 3(r), 7(cr), 9(bl), 25(b), 23(all); M-Press Picture Library: 21(r); Performing Arts Library/Clive Barda: 3(l), 19(l); Photostage/Donald Cooper: 12(b), 18; Stanton Collection: 15; Trustees of the National Library of Scotland: 9(tr); Victoria & Albert Museum, London: 9(tl); Zefa: 22.

All illustrations and symbols: John See